50 BRITISH RECIPES

Cookbook from Authentic British Chefs

Catherine Steele

CONTENTS

50 BRITISH RECIPES:
COOKBOOK
FROM AUTHENTIC
BRITISH CHEFS

INTRODUCTION

British or English cuisine has a reputation for being one thing above all else: heavy, greasy and largely tasteless. For a long time you could believe that everything is eaten here - as long as it is fried and served with French fries - the so-called "fries". In the supermarkets you often looked in vain for fresh ingredients between the endless shelves with frozen and microwave dishes, and even today young English people in particular seem to have no idea how to prepare dishes without a microwave.

On the other hand, the English swear by their classics: on the traditional Sunday Roast with roast beef, Yorkshire pudding, roast potatoes and vegetables, on the sandwich that celebrated its 250th birthday in 2012, on jacket potatoes, baked potatoes that are easy to find in all imaginable variations and let it be prepared quickly, the classic English breakfast, which demands a lot from the European stomach early in the morning, on your pies, pasties and pies. Together with fish & chips, these dishes are still an integral part of English cuisine today. They can be found on every menu in every pub, restaurant, British shop and also on every family menu.

HOW ENGLISH CUISINE GOT ITS REPUTATION

The reputation of English cuisine was not always so bad: in the 19th century, cuisine anglaise stood for particularly refined, exquisite culinary art, for good taste and a high level of culinary culture. As the largest colonial power on earth, England had access to the most exotic ingredients, extraordinary spices and the culinary art of the colonized countries.

The influence of the Commonwealth of Nations - especially China and India - can still be felt very clearly today. Curries - especially the inevitable chicken tikka masala - have become as an integral part of English cuisine as is Yorkshire pudding or its Christmas cousin, plum pudding.

The decline of English cuisine then went hand in hand with the end of the colonial era. After the First World War, fewer and fewer British people could afford the luxury of domestic servants, who at that time were primarily responsible for cooking. The cooks in the high houses were the bearers of English culinary art, the experts for exquisite cuisine Anglaise. When they lost their jobs, they lost access to the ingredients.

And so a situation arose from which English cuisine has not yet fully recovered: Those who had the know-how did not have the ingredients and those who had the ingredients could not cook. That was the end of English cuisine, as it was touted around the world in the 19th century.

For almost 80 years, English cuisine had to put up with being decried as barely edible. Only the royal cucumber sandwich and the Sunday roast were remnants of the once high art of cooking, even if they have since become trivialized without equal. The sandwich is still an integral part of British tea culture, which has also survived over the years and plays a role especially in aristocratic circles - and in those who would like to be.

THE SANDWICH AND ITS STORY...

The sandwich is now the most popular snack in English cuisine, is part of the traditional picnic and is eaten by the British when they travel. The sandwich is named after the fourth Earl of Sandwich, John Montagu, who was a passionate card player and couldn't find time for a snack during a cribbage game that lasted for hours in 1762.

According to legend, he asked to have his food served between two slices of bread so that he had one hand free to play while he ate his snack with the other hand. When one of his teammates asked for a "bread like sandwich", the sandwich was born.

It is the forerunner of the fast kitchen, of burgers and Co., which you simply cannot avoid in England and which you can quickly pick up anywhere. In restaurants, the sandwich is usually served with a little salad and crisps on the side. Crisps are potato chips that are offered in quick English cuisine as an equivalent alternative to potatoes or mashed potatoes. The small bags of crisps that can be found in every snack bar are equally popular with all age groups - and are one of the reasons why English cuisine is considered so extremely unhealthy and greasy.

THE NEW ENGLISH CUISINE FOR CONNOISSEURS

Jacket potatoes are favorites in English cuisine: simple and straightforward.

But that is now slowly coming to an end. Young, innovative, creative chefs - among whom Jamie Oliver is probably the best known - give English cuisine a new face and thus help it to finally break away from its bad image. But the young chefs by no means do without the classics, which they reinterpret in a detoxified, light form and thus make you want to feast and enjoy. Tradition and innovation stand side by side in the English kitchen without disturbing each other. Refined new creations with regional and seasonal ingredients enrich the menus, which were otherwise a common heap of mostly very fatty dishes throughout the country.

THE NEW ENGLISH CUISINE IS LIGHTER AND HEALTHIER - THIS ALSO APPLIES TO FISH AND CHIPS.

Here you can experience English cuisine at its best, enjoy excellent lamb dishes (e.g. with mint sauce, a real delicacy!), Tender Aberdeen Angus beef, smoked fish from the north-west of Scotland , delicious seafood freshly prepared and the more than 700 locals Cheeses, of which Stilton, Cheddar and Gloucester are the most famous. Even fish & chips is no longer greasy cod floating in vinegar, but delicious haddock, freshly caught plaice or even rays or halibut, coated with a crispy, light-weight batter and served with select fresh vegetables.

THE CLOTTED CREAM IS A DELIGHT IN ENGLISH CUISINE.

And when you think of the desserts and sweet delicacies that English cuisine has to offer, your mouth will definitely water: scones with orange jam and clotted cream from Cornwall for tea, brownies, fruit cakes, chocolate fudge, crumble and Cupcakes make the hearts of connoisseurs beat faster.

So give English cuisine a chance and let it convince you. The so-called gastro pubs, a trend from London, are particularly suitable for this. The gastro-pubs combine modern pub culture with high culinary art and come up with a menu that elicits exclamations of happiness even from discerning gourmets. Of course, you can also experiment with the recipes of English cuisine at home.

There are more than enough suggestions for this. Bring a little bit of Great Britain home with you and look forward to your next vacation in England.

ENGLISH FOOD CULTURE

The English are best known for their rich English breakfast. Black pudding, jam, eggs and muesli are served with toast with salted butter. The most famous variant combines toast with fried eggs, baked beans in tomato sauce, sausages and fried tomatoes. Since many people in England used to be into agriculture, a fortifying breakfast was necessary for a day of hard work in the fields.

However, the preparation of such a rich breakfast is very complex and time-consuming, which is why the English rarely cook it at home these days. In the morning there is too little time in the office before work and, like us, only a quick breakfast with toast and cereal is eaten. For this reason, the Full English Breakfast should not be missing on the menus of hotels, cafés and snack bars.

English Sunday dinner: Sunday Roast

Many households still have the Sunday Roast on Sunday. Then the real dishes are served and there are delicacies from the English kitchen, such as roast lamb, beef, pork and roasted potatos,

Yorkshire pudding, peas, parsnips, green beans and so on. Popular sauces are the mint sauce with lamb and an apple sauce with pork. Beef is refined with a horseradish sauce.

Then there is a sweet snack for dessert. English cuisine has countless delicious desserts to offer. This includes the traditional rice pudding (rice pudding), trifle and warm cake with vanilla ice cream or vanilla sauce (custard). The dessert itself is called pudding in English, which often causes irritation for us when no conventional pudding is on the table.

Popular ingredients in English cuisine are potatoes, lamb and fish. Potatoes to mash (mashed potatos), baked potatoes, fried potatoes and chips processed and eaten in stews and savory cakes. There is an abundance of fish on the island and its residents get really creative with plaice, haddock and salmon in the kitchen. It is served in soups, pies and in a deep fried crust.

ENGLISH CUISINE: TEA TIME

The national drink of the English is of course tea. Even if today people are no longer invited to the stately tea time at 5 o'clock sharp, the English still celebrate tea drinking. There is the traditional afternoon tea, early morning tea, breakfast tea and the high tea, which is drunk in the evening. Preferably, of course, in the form of strong black tea that is poured loosely into the pot and repeatedly poured over with hot water. The combination with milk takes some getting used to, but makes the tea milder and creamy.

The English also like to have a snack. The sandwich is probably the most English snack par excellence and was allegedly invented by the fourth Earl of Sandwich, who had his meal sandwiched between two loaves of bread so that he could have one hand free while playing cards. After that, the "bread like sandwich" became widely known and loved by the nobility. Another version is that the Earl didn't want to take a break from working at his desk to eat, so he invented the sandwich.

Today the sandwich in all variations, whether with cheddar, ham, smoked fish or a slice of roast beef, is a popular meal for on the go and an indispensable part of afternoon tea. Lettuce, tomatoes and cucumbers should not be missing on the bread. But also scones with strawberry jam clotted cream (a kind of thick cream), cupcakes, crumble, toffees and pies are popular bites with tea.

In the evening it can be something with percentages. Many English regions have their own beer, which the pubs like to drink after work. Popular alcoholic drinks in England are:

- Real ale
- Guinness
- Lager beer
- gin
- Cider
- port wine

ENGLISH SPECIALTIES AND DISHES

For a long time, England's cuisine was considered inedible and unimaginative. They were associated with fatty and oily foods that are best fried, such as the well-known fish and chips and the excessive use of vinegar. But English cuisine is gradually recovering from this bad reputation and is enjoying an upswing thanks to international influences and the work of young English chefs.

Hearty home cooking from traditional dishes meet exotic flavors from former colonies such as India. This is why English classics such as roast beef are just as popular as curries. Chicken Tikka Masala is no longer considered an immigrant dish, but is an integral part of English cuisine.

The countless English pies and pasties are also famous. In England, pies are particularly popular as savory pies. They consist of a filling of, for example, minced meat and potatoes or chicken and mushrooms, which is slumbering under a batter. Vegetables and fish are also often coated in dough in English cuisine. Pasties are small, handy puff pastries filled with meat and vegetables that are often eaten on the go.

Cheddar is used in dishes and on sandwiches. The hard cheese comes from the island and is named after a village in south-west England. Traditionally it has a very long ripening period, which can stretch to two years. Cheddar is mentioned for the first time in writing as early as 1655. Of the small English bread rolls called scones, there is also a popular variant with cheddar, the cheese scones.

MORE TYPICAL ENGLISH SPECIALTIES

- Yorkshire pudding is a type of pastry made from flour, milk, eggs, fat and spices that is served as an accompaniment to meat dishes. If you bake it in pie molds, a hollow is created on its surface, into which the gravy is filled. If you granulate the Yorkshire pudding with sugar syrup or jam, you can serve it as a dessert.
- Stew is the same as our stew and can combine a variety of ingredients from potatoes, carrots and beans to beef, sausages and seafood. Instead of water, beer, wine or cider can also be used as a soup base.
- For Toad in the Hole, sausages are baked in a baking dish in Yorkshire pudding.
- Bangers and mash is a simple dish made from fried sausages made from pork, beef or lamb and mashed potatoes. Peas are eaten for this purpose, for example.
- Lancashire Hot Pot is a lamb and onion stew that is covered with potato slices and then baked in the oven.
- Fudge is a soft, sweet caramel confection.
- Mince pies are small pastry cakes made from short crust or puff pastry that are filled with fruits and nuts and seasoned with cinnamon and nutmeg. They are mainly eaten at Christmas time.
- For crumble, fruits are sprinkled with crumble and then baked in the oven. The best known is the Apple Crumble.

CIDER PORK

Servings: 4

INGREDIENTS

- 2 large onions
- 1-2 Garlic cloves
- 5 slices Breakfast bacon

- 1.2 kg Potatoes
- 4 Pork neck steaks (approx. 180 g each)
- salt and pepper
- 2-3 tbsp oil
- nutmeg
- 1/4 l Cider

PREPARATION

Peel the onions and cut them into rings. Peel garlic and chop finely. Cut the bacon into small cubes. Peel, wash and slice the potatoes.

Wash the meat and pat dry. Season with salt, pepper and garlic. Heat oil in a large pan. Fry the meat vigorously on both sides.

Mix the potatoes and onions. Season well with salt, pepper and nutmeg. Layer about 2/3 of the potatoes in an ovenproof saucepan. Place the meat slices on top, overlapping. Cover with remaining potatoes and sprinkle with bacon.

Pour the cider on top.

Cover and bake in the preheated oven (electric stove: 150 ° C / convection: 125 ° C / gas: level 1) for about 3 hours. After about 2 hours, remove the lid and finish baking.

Drink tip: cool cider (sparkling apple wine).

APPLE WALNUT PIE RECIPE

Servings: 16

INGREDIENTS

- 1.7 kg tart apples (e.g. Granny Smith)
- Juice of 1/2 lemon
- 125 g + 150 g sugar
- 1 packet vanilla sugar
- 1 packet Custard powder
- Fat and flour
- 100 g Walnut kernels
- 325 g Flour
- salt
- Egg yolk (size M)
- 175 g cold butter
- tbsp Breadcrumbs
- Aluminum foil

PREPARATION

Peel and quarter the apples and cut out the cores. Halve the apple quarters, cut into pieces. Bring the apples, 1/2 l water, lemon juice, 125 g sugar and vanilla sugar to the boil. Cover and simmer for 3–5 minutes, depending on the type of apple, until soft but not yet disintegrated.

Mix the pudding powder with 5 tablespoons of cold water until smooth. Pour apples into a colander, catching the liquid. Drain the apples. Measure out 400 ml of liquid, bring to the boil and stir in the mixed pudding powder.

While stirring at least

Simmer for 1 minute. Fold in the apple pieces. Let cool down for about 2 hours.

Grease a pie or spring form pan (approx. 26 cm Ø) and dust with flour. Finely chop the nuts. Knead flour, 150 g sugar, 1 pinch of salt, egg yolk, nuts and butter in flakes first with the dough hook of the mixer, then quickly knead with your hands to make crumbles.

Preheat the oven (electric stove: 200 ° C / convection: 175 ° C / gas: level 3). Press 2/3 of the crumble into the mold to form a base, pressing up an approx. 3 cm high edge. Sprinkle the bottom with breadcrumbs.

Spread the apple compote on top. Spread the remaining crumble on the compote. Bake in a hot oven for 55–60 minutes. Cover with aluminum foil approx. 15 minutes before the end of the baking time. Let cool down. Crème fraîche tastes good with it.

BAKED POLLACK FILLET WITH PEA PUREE, TARTAR SAUCE AND WEDGES (POTATO WEDGES)

Servings: 4

INGREDIENTS

- 800 g Potatoes
- 100 g Flour
- 75 g food starch
- 1/2 tsp baking powder
- 1-2 tbsp Lemon juice
- salt
- 600 g Pollack fillet
- 1 1/2 kg Frying fat
- onion
- 50 g butter or margarine
- 500 g frozen peas
- 200 ml Vegetable broth
- 4 stem (s) mint
- pepper
- Sweet paprika
- oil

PREPARATION

Peel and wash the potatoes, cut into wedges and spread out flat on an oil-coated baking sheet. Bake in a preheated oven (electric stove: 200 ° C / convection: 175 ° C / gas: level 3) for about 40 minutes.

Turn once in between. Mix flour, starch and baking powder for the batter. Stir flour mixture and 180 ml water until smooth. Season with lemon juice and 1 teaspoon salt. Wash the fish, pat dry and cut into portions

Heat the oil in a saucepan (or deep fryer) to 180 ° C. Pull the fish through the batter and fry in portions in the hot frying fat for about 5 minutes. In the meantime, peel and dice the onion. Heat the fat and sauté the onion cubes until translucent.

Add the peas and stock, bring to the boil and simmer for about 5 minutes. Puree to puree with a hand blender. Wash the mint, shake dry, pluck the leaves from the stems and cut into small pieces except for something to garnish.

Season with salt and pepper and season with mint. Mix 1–2 teaspoons of salt and 1 teaspoon of paprika and season the potatoes. A rrange on plates. Remoulade tastes good with it.

LEMON SQUARES
PORK

Servings: 24

INGREDIENTS

- 150 g butter
- 225 g sugar
- grated zest of 3 untreated lemons
- 1 pinch salt
- 175 g Flour
- 4th Eggs (size M)
- 125 g Double cream
- Juice of 3 lemons (approx. 175 ml)
- 1 tbsp powdered sugar
- fat

PREPARATION

Put butter with 25 g sugar, zest of 1/2 lemon, salt and flour in a bowl. First knead with the dough hook of the hand mixer, then with your hands to form a smooth dough. Grease a tightly fitting, square springform pan (24 x 24 cm). Pour the batter in and press it with your hands to a flat bottom. Chill for about 30 minutes

Bake the bottom in a preheated oven (electric stove: 175 ° C / convection: 150 ° C / gas: level 2) for 20-25 minutes until golden brown. Let cool down. In the meantime, stir the eggs and 200 g sugar with the whisk of the hand mixer for about 5 minutes until thick and creamy. Stir in the double cream. Stir the lemon juice and the remaining grated zest into the egg cream

Pour lemon cream on the bottom. Bake in the oven at the same temperature for 20-25 minutes. Let cool on a wire rack. Cut the cake into approx. 24 pieces and dust with powdered sugar

Waiting time approx. 1 1/2 hours

SHEPARD'S PIE

Servings: 4

INGREDIENTS

- 300 g Potatoes
- salt
- small head of cauliflower

- 500 g Beef hip
- Carrots
- small broccoli
- Red onion
- stem (s) parsley
- handle (s) thyme
- tbsp oil
- 1 tsp Tomato paste
- level tablespoon flour
- 200 ml beef broth
- 1 tbsp Worcestershire sauce
- pepper
- 1/2 bunch Spring onions
- 50 g Reduced-fat cream cheese (21% fat in dry matter)
- grated nutmeg

PREPARATION

Peel, wash and chop the potatoes. Cook the potatoes in a large pot in salted water for about 20 minutes until soft. Cut the cauliflower into small florets and add to the potatoes about 10 minutes before the end of the cooking time

Cut the meat into hazelnut-sized cubes. Peel, wash and cut the carrots into pieces. Cut the broccoli into small florets. Peel onion and chop finely. Wash the parsley and thyme, shake dry and finely chop the leaves, except for 2 stalks of parsley

Heat oil in a pan. Sear the meat in it while turning, remove. Put the carrots in the pan and fry them. Add onion cubes and fry for about 1 minute. Stir in tomato paste and fry briefly. Scatter the flour on top and mix well. Add the stock while stirring. Add broccoli, Worcestershire sauce, thyme, parsley and meat and simmer for about 10 minutes. Season with salt and pepper

Wash, clean and finely chop the spring onions. Drain the cauliflower and potatoes. Add the cream cheese and mash to a puree. Add spring onions and season with salt, pepper and nutmeg

Put the beef ragout in an ovenproof dish and spread the puree over it. Spread butter over it and bake in the preheated oven (electric stove: 200 ° C / convection: 175 ° C / gas: level 3) for 20–30 minutes. Take out the pie and garnish with parsley

FISH 'N' CHIPS

Servings: 4

INGREDIENTS

- 750 g Potatoes
- a little oil (e.g. from the spray bottle) + 2 tablespoons of oil

- salt
- pepper
- small onion
- Pickled cucumbers (jar)
- 1/2 bunch chives
- handle (s) parsley
- tbsp light salad cream
- 150 g Skimmed milk yogurt
- 1 tsp medium hot mustard
- 600 g Fish fillet (e.g. ling fish or saithe)
- 1 tbsp Lemon juice
- 2 tbsp Flour
- Parchment paper

PREPARATION

Wash the potatoes well, pat dry and cut into wedges. Place on a baking tray covered with baking paper. Sprinkle with some oil. Season with salt and pepper. Bake in the preheated oven (electric oven: 200 ° C / fan: 175 ° C / gas: level 3) for 45–50 minutes.

Peel and finely dice the onion. Finely dice the cucumber. Wash herbs and shake dry. Cut the chives into fine rolls, chop the parsley. Mix everything with the salad cream, yogurt and mustard

Season to taste with salt and pepper.

Wash the fish, pat dry and cut into bite-sized pieces. Drizzle with lemon juice and season with salt. Turn the fish in flour.

Heat 2 tablespoons of oil in a coated pan. Fry the fish in it for 4–5 minutes, turning. Serve the fish and potato pieces in portions with tartar sauce.

DESSERT: SUMMER PUDDING

Servings: 4

INGREDIENTS

- 900 g frozen, mixed berries (e.g. strawberries, black currants, raspberries, blackberries)
- 1 packet Vanillin sugar
- 200-300 g sugar
- 250 g toast
- Cling film

PREPARATION

Put the frozen berries, 3 tablespoons of water, vanilla sugar and sugar in a saucepan and bring to the boil. In the meantime, remove the crust from the toast. Drain the berries while collecting the juice. Soak slices of toast one after the other with the drained juice and completely line the bottom and walls of a large cup (approx. 300 ml) with it. Hold back enough bread to cover the surface. Put the berries in the cups. Soak the rest of the toast and top with the berries. Wrap the cups in cling film, weigh them down with a board. Let it steep for at least 8 hours in a cool place. Remove the foil, turn the pudding out onto a plate, decorate with lemon balm and berries. Liquid cream tastes good with it

VANILLA SCONES WITH ORANGE KUMQUAT JAM

Servings: 12

INGREDIENTS

- Vanilla pod
- 250 g Flour
- 50 g sugar
- 1 pinch salt
- 1/2 packet baking powder
- 100 g butter
- 125 ml + 2 tbsp milk
- 150 g Mascarpone
- 150 g Double cream
- Flour
- Cling film
- Parchment paper

PREPARATION

Cut the vanilla pod lengthways. Scrape out the pith with the back of a knife. Mix the flour, sugar, vanilla pulp, salt and baking powder in a bowl. Add the butter in flakes and 125 ml milk, knead with the dough hook of the hand mixer to form a smooth dough. Wrap in foil and refrigerate for about 30 minutes. Then let it rest for about 30 minutes at room temperature

Knead the dough well again with floured hands. Roll out about 1.5 cm thick on a floured work surface. Cut out circles (6 cm Ø). Place on a baking sheet lined with parchment paper. Knead the rest of the dough again and cut out a total of 12 circles

Brush the dough circles with 2 tablespoons of milk and bake in the preheated oven (electric stove: 200 ° C / convection: 175 ° C / gas: level 3) for 12-14 minutes. Take out and place on a wire rack. In the meantime, mix the mascarpone and crème double together for the creme. Scones taste best when they are lukewarm. Add the cream and orange kumquat jam

SMOKY CHEDDAR BURGER

Servings: 6

INGREDIENTS

- 2 lb. baking potatoes, scrubbed and pierced
- Tbs. seasoning mix, like Montreal steak seasoning
- lb. ground beef
- Tbs. steak marinade, like A1
- 6th slices of smoked cheddar cheese
- 6th slices bacon, cooked till crisp
- ½ small red onion, sliced
- cup of mayonnaise
- ½ cup minced roasted red pepper
- clove garlic, minced
- lemon, zested and juiced
- ½ tsp. Dijon mustard
- 6 hamburger buns
- 6 leaves Boston lettuce
- 6 slices tomato

PREPARATION

Heat oven to 400 ° F. Place potatoes in microwave and cook on high power 5 min. Remove, let cool 5 min. Cut into wedges. Place on foil lined greased baking sheet. Coat with cooking spray. Sprinkle with half the seasoning mix. Bake 10 min. Turn wedges, spray and sprinkle with remaining seasoning mix. Beacon 5 min

In bowl, whisk together mayonnaise, red pepper, garlic, ¼ tsp. lemon zest, 1 tsp. lemon juice and ½ tsp. Dijon mustard

Heat grill. Grill buns briefly to toast. In bowl, combine beef and marinade. Shape into 6 patties. Cook patties to desired doness. Place cheese over patties 3 min. Before removing from grill

Spread buns with 1 Tbs. mayonnaise mixture. Top with lettuce, tomato, burger, onion slices and bacon. Serve with potato wedges and remaining mayonnaise

LEMON TRIFLE WITH RASPBERRIES

Servings: 4

INGREDIENTS

- untreated lemon
- 100 g Raspberries
- 250 g lowfat quark
- 30 g + 1 tbsp sugar
- 200 g Whipped cream
- 80 g Ladyfingers
- 150 g Lemon curd

PREPARATION

Wash the lemon with hot water, rub dry, peel off the peel in thin strips with a zest zipper. Finely chop the lemon zest, except for something to sprinkle. Halve the fruit and squeeze out the juice. Sort the raspberries. Mix the quark, 30 g sugar, chopped zest and 2 tablespoons lemon juice. Whip the cream until stiff and fold into the cream

Mix the remaining lemon juice, 4 tablespoons of water and 1 tablespoon of sugar. Spread half of the biscuits in a bowl. Drizzle with half the lemon syrup. Spread 1/3 of the cream on top. Spread the remaining biscuits on top and drizzle with the remaining lemon syrup. Spread the raspberries on top except for a few to sprinkle. Cover with approx. 1/3 cream raspberries. Spread half of the lemon curd on top. Spread the rest of the cream and curd on top. Sprinkle with the remaining raspberries and zest. Let it steep in the refrigerator for at least 2 hours

LEMON CURD TARTLETS

Servings: 6

INGREDIENTS

- 110 g butter
- 250 g shortbread
- 2 untreated lemons
- 100 g sugar
- 35 g food starch
- 2 Egg yolk (size M)
- 150 g Raspberries
- oil

PREPARATION

Melt 100 g butter and let cool down a little. Grind shortbread biscuits in the universal chopper. Pour into a bowl and mix with melted butter. Brush 6 tartlet molds (approx. 11 cm Ø) with the lift-off base lightly with oil. Distribute the crumbs in the molds, first press on the edge, then on the bottom. Chill molds for approx. 30 minutes. Wash 1 lemon with hot water, rub dry and rub off the peel. Halve both lemons and squeeze them. Fill up lemon juice with water to 350 ml and bring to the boil in a saucepan with sugar and 10 g butter. Mix the starch with approx. 4 tablespoons of cold water until smooth. Thicken the simmering stock while stirring vigorously and continue to simmer for approx. 1 minute, remove from heat, pour into a bowl and let cool down for 2-3 minutes. Mix egg yolks with 1–2 tablespoons of hot cream. Stir egg mixture into the rest of the cream. Fold in lemon zest. Spread the hot cream in the tartlets and let cool. Sort the raspberries and distribute them on top. Chill the tart for approx. 20 minutes

HEADS OF ASPARAGUS (SOLDIERS) WITH SOFT-BOILED EGG

Servings: 4

INGREDIENTS

- 500 g green asparagus
- salt
- 4th Eggs (size M)
- sea-salt

PREPARATION

Wash the asparagus, cut off the woody ends. Halve the asparagus spears. Cook the asparagus heads in boiling salted water for about 4 minutes. Use the remaining asparagus for other purposes

Cook the eggs in boiling water for about 5 minutes until soft

Arrange asparagus and eggs. Open the eggs, season with sea salt and dip the asparagus tips into the egg yolks

ENGLISH DESSERT

Servings: 6

INGREDIENTS

- 1 glass (720 ml; 370 g) cherries
- 1 package (175 g) Double cream cream cheese
- 250 g Cream curd (40%)

- Egg yolk (size M)
- 400 g Whipped cream
- 100 g + 2 tbsp sugar
- 1 packet Cream stabilizer
- 1 packet Vanillin sugar
- 100 g Flaked almonds
- 1 tbsp butter

PREPARATION

Drain the cherries well. Beat the cream cheese and quark until smooth. Stir in egg yolks, 200 g cream and 100 g sugar. Mix the cream stabilizer and vanilla sugar. Whip 200 g cream until stiff, pour in the whipped cream mixture. Fold the cream into the cream. Pour approx. 1/4 of the cream into a bowl and smooth it out. Spread the cherries on top. Spread the rest of the cream on top, chill

Put the almond flakes, butter and 2 tablespoons sugar in a pan. Heat, stirring, until the almonds are golden brown and the butter has melted. Take out of the pan and let cool down. Sprinkle almonds on top of the cream just before serving

SAUSAGE ROLLS (PUFF PASTRY ROLLS WITH SAUSAGE FILLING)

Servings: 14

INGREDIENTS

- 500 g tomatoes
- 2 large onions
- 1 piece (s) (approx. 40 g) ginger
- red chilli pepper
- 50 g Brown sugar
- tbsp Tomato paste
- salt
- Cayenne pepper
- cumin
- 1-2 tbsp White wine vinegar
- 1 tbsp oil
- stem (s) sage
- 4th coarse sausages (approx. 100 g each)
- 1 tbsp breadcrumbs
- pepper
- grated nutmeg
- 1 package (270 g) Fresh butter puff pastry (ready to bake, rolled out on baking paper; 42 x 24 cm; cooling shelf)
- Egg (size M)
- 100 g Cheddar cheese
- Parchment paper

PREPARATION

For the chutney, wash, clean and dice tomatoes. Peel the onions and finely dice them. Peel the ginger, grate finely. Clean the chilli, cut lengthways, remove the seeds, wash the pod and cut into small pieces

Caramelize the sugar in a saucepan. Add the tomatoes, half of the onions, ginger, chilli and tomato paste. Simmer for about 15 minutes over a medium heat, stirring frequently. Season to taste with salt, cayenne pepper, cumin and vinegar. Let cool down

Heat the oil in a pan and fry the remaining onion cubes over a medium heat until golden brown. Wash the sage, pat dry and finely chop. Add to the onions, set aside and let cool. Press the sausage meat out of the sausage skin. Knead with onions and breadcrumbs. Season with pepper and nutmeg

Take the dough out of the refrigerator 5–10 minutes before processing. Unroll the dough and cut it in half lengthways, creating two rectangles (42 x 12 cm each). Halve the sausage meat. Shape half of the sausage on each half of the dough into a sausage the length of the dough piece. Roll everything up and cut each roll into approx. 7 pieces. Put on baking paper. Use a teaspoon to squeeze the open ends a little

Whisk the egg and brush the puff pastry with it. Coarsely grate the cheese and sprinkle the sausage rolls with it. Bake in a preheated oven (electric stove: 200 ° C / convection: 175 ° C / gas: level 3) for about 20 minutes until golden brown. Serve with the chutney. The rolls taste warm or cold

FISHERMANS PIE (SALMON AND LING FISH PIE)

Servings: 4

INGREDIENTS

- 230 g Flour
- Egg (size M)
- sugar
- salt
- 130 g butter
- 500 g Leeks
- 400 g Salmon and ling fish fillet
- 400 ml milk
- Bay leaves
- pepper
- 150 g frozen young peas
- onion
- 7-8 tbsp dry white wine
- Egg yolk (size M)
- Cling film
- fat
- Flour

PREPARATION

For the short crust pastry, knead 200 g flour, egg, 1 pinch of sugar, 1/2 teaspoon salt and 100 g butter with the dough hook of the hand mixer. Then knead with your hands to form a smooth dough.

Wrap in foil and refrigerate for about 30 minutes. Clean and wash the leek and cut into rings. Wash and pat dry the fish and cut into cubes. Heat the milk, 1 teaspoon salt, bay leaves and pepper in a large saucepan.

Add fish cubes and let simmer for 2-3 minutes over low heat. Carefully lift it out and put the milk aside. Put the leek in boiling salted water and cook for about 5 minutes. Add the peas 1 minute before the end of the cooking time.

Then pour into a sieve, collect the vegetable water and drain well. Measure out 150 ml of vegetable water. Peel onion and chop finely. Heat 30 g butter in a saucepan, sauté the onion in it.

Dust with 30 g flour, sweat and gradually deglaze with the vegetable water and the milk. Boil. Add wine. Season to taste with salt, pepper and sugar. Mix in vegetables. Carefully fold in the fish.

Grease 4 tartar molds (15 cm Ø). Spread the ragout evenly in it. Roll out the shortcrust pastry thinly (approx. 37 x 37 cm) on a floured work surface. Cut out 4 circles (18 cm Ø).

Make a whole (chimney 1.5 cm Ø) in each circle. Place a sheet of dough on each of the tart cases. Press the edge downwards. Knead the remaining dough again, roll out thinly and cut out small fish.

Place the fish on the pastry sheets. Whisk the egg yolk and 1 tbsp water. Brush the dough sheets with it. Bake in a preheated oven (electric stove: 200 ° C / convection: 175 ° C / gas: level 3) for 25–30 minutes. A salad tastes good with it.

SPICY COTTAGE PIE

Servings: 4

INGREDIENTS

- 1-1.2 kg Potatoes (e.g. floury)
- Salt, white pepper
- 1 bunch Soup greens

- 2 medium-sized onions
- 1-2 Garlic cloves
- 750 g according to minced meat
- 1-2 tbsp Oil, sweet paprika
- 1 tbsp Tomato paste
- 1 tsp Broth (instant)
- 300 ml milk
- 1 tbsp Butter / margarine
- grated nutmeg

PREPARATION

Peel, wash and chop the potatoes. Cook in salted water for about 20 minutes

Clean or peel soup greens, wash. Cut the carrots into slices and the remaining vegetables into fine cubes. Peel the onions and garlic. Chop both

Fry the mince in a large pan in the hot oil until crumbly. Season with salt, pepper and paprika. Add onions, garlic and soup greens, fry with. Sweat tomato paste with. Deglaze with 1/4 l water and bring to the boil. Stir in the broth and simmer for 8-10 minutes

Drain and mash the potatoes. Add milk and fat and stir in. Season with salt, pepper and nutmeg. Put the mince in a baking dish. Spread the mashed potatoes on top. Bake in a hot oven (electric stove: 200 ° C / convection: 175 ° C / gas: level 3) for about 20 minutes

FRIED PRAWNS ON TOAST - POLAR SEA PRAWNS ON TOASTED WHITE BREAD

Servings: 6

INGREDIENTS

- 500 g Arctic prawns in brine or cooked and peeled scampi
- Organic lemon
- 1/2 Perennial celery stalk
- onion
- small bunch of parsley
- tbsp butter
- 6 slices White bread
- salt
- pepper

PREPARATION

Drain the prawns well. Wash lemon with hot water and rub dry. Cut the ends, cut the lemon into 6 slices. Clean, wash and slice the celery. Peel onion and chop finely.

Wash the parsley, shake dry and cut the leaves into strips.

Heat 2 tablespoons of butter in a large pan. Briefly toast the bread slices on each side. Take out and put on plate.

Heat the rest of the butter in the frying fat. Steam the onion, celery, prawns and lemon for about 5 minutes while stirring. Remove lemon slices after approx. 2 minutes. Season to taste with salt and pepper

Spread on the bread. Garnish with lemon and parsley.

ONION AND
CUCUMBER PICKLES

Servings:4

INGREDIENTS

- 500 g Vegetable onions
- 1 glass (720 ml) gherkins
- 3 tbsp Sunflower oil
- 2 tsp Mustard seeds
- 3 Bay leaves
- 1 tsp Sweet paprika
- 6 tbsp White wine vinegar
- 5 tbsp Apple juice
- Chilli pepper
- salt
- pepper
- sugar

PREPARATION

Peel the onions and cut them into rings. Pour the pickles into a sieve, collecting the stock. Cut the cucumber into oblique, wide strips. Heat the oil in a pan, fry the onions over medium heat until golden brown. Add mustard seeds, bay leaves and paprika. Add vinegar, apple juice and 5 tablespoons of cucumber stock. Clean and wash the chilli pepper and cut in half lengthways. Remove cores. Cut the pod into fine cubes, add to the stock and simmer for about 10 minutes over medium heat. Add the cucumber, bring to the boil again and season with salt, pepper and sugar. Pour hot into clean twist-off glasses

CHICKEN CLUB SANDWICH

Servings: 4

INGREDIENTS

- clove of garlic
- 4 tbsp olive oil
- tbsp Worcestershire Sauce
- salt
- pepper
- Rose peppers
- 400 g Chicken fillet
- ripe avocado
- 1-2 tbsp Lemon juice
- Cumin
- green pepper sauce
- 8 slices Breakfast bacon
- 8 sheets Lettuce
- Beefsteak tomato
- onion
- 1/2 bunch coriander
- 8 slices Whole wheat sandwich toast

PREPARATION

Peel the garlic and press it through a garlic press. Mix together the oil and Worcestershire sauce and season with salt, pepper, garlic and paprika. Wash the meat, pat dry and turn in the marinade. Chill for about 30 minutes. In the meantime, halve the avocado, remove the stone, remove the pulp from the skin with a spoon and puree. Season savory with salt, lemon juice, cumin and pepper sauce. Remove the chicken fillet from the marinade and stir-fry in a hot pan for about 6 minutes. Take out meat. Fry the bacon in it until crispy. Wash the lettuce and shake dry. Wash and clean the tomato and cut into thin slices. Peel the onion and cut into rings. Wash the coriander and shake dry. Cut the meat n thin slices. Toast bread and brush with avocado cream. Cover 4 slices one after the other with 1 lettuce leaf, meat, 2 tomato slices, onion, coriander, bacon and lettuce each. Finish with the second slice of bread and cut sandwiches in half

ENGLISH STYLE TOAST

Servings: 1

INGREDIENTS

- 3-4 Cornichons (approx. 60 g)
- 2 slices toast
- 2 tbsp remoulade

- 4 slices (20 g each) roast beef
- 3 tbsp (10 g each) grated cheddar cheese
- some stalks of chives
- Parchment paper

PREPARATION

Drain the gherkins and cut into slices. Toast the toast in the toaster until golden brown. Brush with tartar sauce. Roll up the roast beef and place on the toast. Spread the cucumber on top, sprinkle with cheese.

Place the toast on a parchment-lined baking sheet. Bake in the preheated oven (electric stove: 200 ° C / convection: 175 ° C / gas: level 3) for 4-6 minutes until the cheese has melted. Wash the chives, pat dry, cut a few stalks into rolls.

Garnish the toast with chives rolls and stalks.

SALMON TROUT WITH GREEN MAYONNAISE AND HORSERADISH SAUCE

Servings: 4

INGREDIENTS

- large salmon trout (approx. 1 kg)
- tbsp Lemon juice
- salt
- pepper
- 2-3 stem (s) parsley
- small onion
- tbsp dry white wine
- 1 bunch dill
- 200 g Salad mayonnaise
- 5-8 tbsp Whipped cream
- 125 g Double cream
- 1-2 tbsp grated horseradish (glass)
- 1 pinch sugar
- 1 tbsp Chives rolls for sprinkling
- Lemon wedges
- fat
- Aluminum foil

PREPARATION

\Wash the salmon trout inside and out under running water and pat dry. Add 1-2 tablespoons of lemon juice, salt and pepper to the abdominal cavity. Grease a large piece of aluminum foil and place the trout on top.

Wash the parsley and shake dry. Peel and quarter the onion. Drizzle the trout with white wine and the remaining lemon juice. Spread the onions and parsley around the fish. Fold the aluminum foil over the fish from two sides to make an airy, well-sealed package.

Place the parcel diagonally on a baking sheet and stew in the preheated oven (electric stove: 175 ° C / convection: 150 ° C / gas: level 2) for 30-40 minutes. In the meantime, wash the dill for the dill mayonnaise, shake dry and put 2 stalks aside for garnish.

Finely chop the rest of the dill. Mix together the mayonnaise and dill and puree with a cutting stick. Stir in the cream and season with salt and pepper. For the horseradish sauce, mix the crème double and the horseradish together and season with sugar, salt and pepper.

Arrange the horseradish sauce in a sauce boat and sprinkle with chives. Chill both sauces. Take the finished trout out of the oven. Carefully remove the skin and head and arrange the trout on a platter.

Let cool down completely. Just before serving, pour some dill mayonnaise over the cold trout, sprinkle with lemon wedges and the rest of the dill and garnish. Add the rest of the sauces.

Fresh white bread and salad go well with this.

ROAST TURKEY À LA WELLINGTON

Servings: 4

INGREDIENTS

- 5 medium-sized onions
- 1 kg Turkey breast
- Salt, pepper, 2 tablespoons of oil
- 3/8 - 1/2 l Chicken broth (instant)
- 4 slices (75 g each) Frozen puff pastry
- 500 g Mushrooms
- 1/2 Bunch / pot of basil and parsley
- Egg + 1 yolk
- 50 g breadcrumbs
- 1 kg Pointed cabbage, 2 carrots
- 1 tbsp Butter / margarine
- Nutmeg, 1 tbsp cornstarch
- Parchment paper

PREPARATION

Peel the onions. Quarter 2 onions. Wash meat, pat dry. Season with salt and pepper. Heat 1 tablespoon of oil in the roasting pan. Fry the meat all over. Fry the onion quarters briefly. Pour in the broth. Cover and simmer for 30-40 minutes. Remove the roast and let it cool for 30 minutes. Sieve the stock, set aside

Thaw the dough. Finely dice 2 onions. Clean, wash and finely chop the mushrooms. Fry with the onions in 1 tablespoon of hot oil. Fry for about 10 minutes until all the liquid has evaporated

Wash and chop herbs. Mix with the mushroom mixture, egg and breadcrumbs, season. Place 2 slices of dough on top of each other and roll out to the size of the roast. Place on the baking tray lined with baking paper. Brush with half of the mushroom mixture. Place the meat on top and brush with the remaining mushroom mixture

Place the remaining dough slices on top of each other and roll out to the size of the roast. Roll over it with a wire mesh roller (or cut the dough into strips). Pull the grid apart and place it over the roast. Press the edges firmly on. Mix the egg yolk and 1 tbsp water. Brush the dough with it

Bake the roast in the hot oven (electric oven: 200 ° C / convection:

175 ° C / gas: level 3) on the lower rack for about 45 minutes

Clean and wash pointed cabbage. Remove the stalk. Cut the cabbage into small pieces. Peel, wash and slice the carrots. Dice the remaining onion and sauté in the hot fat. Briefly sauté the pointed cabbage and carrots. Cover and cook in 1/8 l water for about 10 minutes. Season with salt and nutmeg

Bring the stock to the boil and reduce for approx. 5 minutes. Mix the starch with a little water until smooth. Bind the stock with it. To taste. Serve everything

ROAST BEEF WITH CUMBERLAND SAUCE

Servings: 4

INGREDIENTS

- 500 g frozen peas
- 5 tbsp dry red wine
- heaped teaspoon cornstarch
- 6 tbsp red currant jelly
- 2-3 tsp hot mustard
- grated zest of 1 untreated orange and 1 lemon each
- Juice of 2 oranges and 1 lemon
- 5 tbsp port wine
- salt
- Sweet paprika
- 1 kg Potatoes
- 1 kg roast beef
- pepper
- 2-3 tbsp Clarified butter
- 1 pinch sugar
- parsley
- fat

PREPARATION

Thaw the peas. For the sauce, stir together the red wine and starch until smooth. Dissolve the jelly in a saucepan, stirring constantly. Stir in mustard, orange and lemon zest. Stir until smooth and mix with orange and lemon juice and port wine.

Bring to the boil, add the starch while stirring and bring to the boil again. Season the sauce with salt and paprika, leave to cool. Wash potatoes and cook in water for 15-20 minutes. Then rinse in cold water, peel and let rest.

In the meantime, wash the roast beef and pat dry. Season with salt and pepper. Place on a greased baking sheet and fry in the preheated oven (electric stove: 200 ° C / fan: 175 ° C / gas: level 3) for 35-40 minutes.

Heat 1 tablespoon of clarified butter. Fry the potatoes all around over a medium heat for about 8 minutes. Season with salt and pepper. Blanch the peas for 3-4 minutes in a little boiling water, drain and drain.

Heat 1-2 tablespoons clarified butter in a saucepan. Swirl the peas in it. Season with salt and sugar. Remove the roast beef. Let rest for 5 minutes, cut open and serve with vegetables, potatoes and sauce.

Serve garnished with parsley.

SADDLE OF LAMB WITH MINT SAUCE

Servings: 4

INGREDIENTS

- 350 g Potatoes
- salt
- 1 kg Saddle of lamb
- pepper
- onion
- 1 piece (s) (approx. 20 g) ginger
- 1/2 tsp Sweet paprika
- tbsp Lemon juice
- tbsp honey
- 1 tbsp oil
- 30 g butter
- 90 g Flour
- 1/2 tsp baking powder
- some Milk
- 30 g Clarified butter
- 2 Peppermint stem
- 2 tbsp whiskey
- 1 tbsp vinegar
- sugar
- Flour

PREPARATION

Peel and wash the potatoes and cook in salted boiling water for about 20 minutes. In the meantime, wash the meat and pat dry. Incise the skin of the saddle of lamb in a diamond shape. Rub with pepper and place on the oven pan.

Fry in a preheated oven (electric stove: 200 ° C / gas: level 3) for about 40 minutes. Peel and finely chop the onions and ginger. Mix with 1/2 teaspoon each of salt and paprika, lemon juice, honey and oil.

Brush the saddle of lamb with the marinade approx. 15 minutes before the end of the cooking time. Drain the potatoes and let them cool down a little. Melt the butter. Put the flour, salt and baking powder in a bowl. Press the potatoes through a potato press or pound them finely.

Add to the flour mixture, add butter and mix everything into a smooth dough. If the dough is too firm, add a little milk if necessary. Sprinkle a work surface with flour. Halve the dough, roll out into two circles (each approx. 14 cm Ø)

Cut the dough circles into 6 pieces each. Fry the potato wedges in hot clarified butter until golden brown. Take the saddle of lamb out of the oven and keep warm. Sieve the meat stock and add 1/4 liter of water. Bring to the boil and simmer over low heat for 5 minutes.

Wash the mint, pluck the leaves and finely chop except for a few for garnish. Add the whiskey, vinegar and mint to the sauce. Add sugar and salt to taste. Arrange the saddle of lamb and potato wedges on a platter.

Garnish with mint. Serve the sauce separately. Beans and grilled tomatoes taste great with it.

CORNISH PASTY

Servings: 13

INGREDIENTS

450 g Flour

- salt

- 100 g butter
- 100 g Lard (alternatively 100 g butter)
- 300 g Potatoes
- 125 g Carrots
- onion
- 150 g lean beef steak
- 1 tsp Instant vegetable broth
- pepper
- sugar
- Egg yolk (size M)
- tbsp milk
- Flour
- Parchment paper
- Wooden skewers

PREPARATION

Mix the flour and a teaspoon of salt. Add the butter and lard in flakes and knead well with the dough hook of the hand mixer. Then knead again well with your hands. Cover and chill for 45 minutes. In the meantime, peel, wash and finely dice the potatoes and carrots for the filling. Peel the onion and dice very finely. Wash the meat, pat dry and finely dice. For the filling, mix the meat, potatoes, carrots, onion and stock. Season well with salt, pepper and sugar. Shape the dough into a roll and cut into 13 slices. Roll out each disc into a circle (approx. 14.5 cm) on a floured work surface. Brush the edges with water. Spread the filling evenly on top, leaving a 1.5 centimeter wide border. Fold the dough circle over and press together. Place on two baking sheets lined with baking paper and prick several times with a wooden skewer. Whisk the egg yolks and milk together. Brush the dumplings with it. Bake one after the other in a preheated oven (electric stove: 225 ° C / fan: 200 ° C / gas: level 4) for 20 minutes. Then reduce the baking temperature to (electric stove: 150 ° C / convection: 125 ° C / gas: level 1) and bake for another 20 minutes. Take out of the oven and serve

RASPBERRY AND RHUBARB CRUMBLE

Servings: 4

INGREDIENTS

- 200 g Flour
- 100 g sugar
- 100 g cold butter
- 1 packet Vanillin sugar
- 1 pinch salt
- Egg (size S)
- 300 g rhubarb
- 250 g frozen raspberries
- fat
- Aluminum foil

PREPARATION

Put the flour, sugar, flaky butter, vanilla sugar, salt and egg in a large bowl. Mix with the dough hook of the hand mixer. Then work with your hands into crumbles. Grease a rectangular tart pan (26 cm x 19 cm x 3 cm). Clean and wash the rhubarb and cut into pieces approx. 2 cm wide. Pour the rhubarb and raspberries into the pan and sprinkle the crumble on top. Bake in the preheated oven (electric stove: 200 ° C / convection: 175 ° C / gas: level 3) for about 45 minutes on the lower rail. Cover with aluminum foil approx. 15 minutes before the end of the baking time. Take out of the oven, place on a rack and let cool down a little

SCONES (TEA CAKES)

Servings: 20

INGREDIENTS

- 500 g Flour
- 2 packages baking powder
- 125 g sugar

- 125 g soft butter
- 125-150 ml + 2-3 tbsp milk
- egg yolk
- Flour
- Parchment paper

PREPARATION

Briefly knead the flour, baking powder, sugar and butter. Gradually knead in 125-150 ml milk and work it into a smooth dough. Roll out the dough 1-2 cm thick on a floured work surface.

Cut out 20 circles (5 cm Ø). Place on a baking tray covered with baking paper. Whisk the egg yolks and 2-3 tablespoons of milk together. Brush the scones with it. Bake in the preheated oven (electric stove: 200 ° C / convection: 175 ° C / gas: level 3) for 10-12 minutes.

Serve the scones with jam and double cream or butter.

FRUITCAKE (FRUIT CAKE)

Servings: 32

INGREDIENTS

- 2 Bag (250 g each) mixed exotic dried fruits (e.g .: papaya, mango, pineapple, kumquats)
- 250 g soft butter
- 175 g Brown sugar
- 1 pinch salt
- Egg (size M)
- Egg yolk (size M)
- 400 g Flour
- 1 packet baking powder
- 1 level tsp cinnamon
- 1 knife point mace
- 6 tbsp orange juice
- powdered sugar
- Fat and breadcrumbs

PREPARATION

Chop the fruits. Mix butter, sugar and salt until creamy. Gradually stir in the egg and yolks. Mix the flour, baking powder and spices, sieve on top and stir in. Stir in the orange juice as well. Fold in the chopped fruits. Grease a loaf pan (25 cm long) well and sprinkle with breadcrumbs. Pour in the dough and smooth it out. Bake in the preheated oven (electric stove: 200 ° C / convection: 175 ° C / gas: level 3) for 1-1 1/4 hours. If it gets too dark, cover with parchment or baking paper. Then let it cool down in the mold for about 10 minutes. Then fall and let cool down completely. Shortly before serving, first cut into approx. 8 thick slices, then cut each slice into 4 cubes. Dust with powdered sugar

TRIFLE

Servings: 4

INGREDIENTS

- 750 g Apples
- 6-7 tbsp Lemon juice
- 90 g sugar

- 8 (approx. 75 g) Ladyfingers
- 4 tbsp Raspberry jam
- 4 tbsp sherry
- 375 ml milk
- 2 level tsp food starch
- egg yolk
- 1/2 tsp Vanilla extract

PREPARATION

Peel and quarter the apples, cut out the core. Cut the pulp into cubes and drizzle with lemon juice. Mix with 75 g of sugar and 8 tablespoons of water in a saucepan. Cover and simmer for 8-10 minutes. Roughly break the biscuits and divide them into 4 large glasses. Heat the jam, stir in the sherry and drizzle on the biscuits. Let it steep for about 1/2 hour at room temperature. In the meantime, stir 100 ml milk and starch in a saucepan until smooth. Add 275 ml milk and 15 g sugar while stirring and bring to the boil. Whisk the egg yolks and 3 tablespoons of the sauce and use the whisk to whisk into the rest of the sauce. Cook for 1 minute, stirring constantly, remove from heat and add vanilla extract. Divide the apple compote in portions into the glasses. Drizzle with vanilla sauce. Suffice the rest of the sauce

PLUM PUDDING

Servings: 12

INGREDIENTS

- 70 g Prunes
- 175 g Raisins
- 1 tbsp rum

- Apple
- 50 g Lemon peel
- 50 g Orange peel
- 60 g breadcrumbs
- 50 g Flour
- 50 g butter or margarine
- 35 g Brown sugar
- Juice and grated zest of 1 untreated lemon
- Eggs (size M)
- 1 pinch ground pepper, nutmeg, cloves, cinnamon and ginger
- 50 g ground hazelnuts
- 500 ml milk
- 25 g sugar
- 1 packet "Vanilla Flavor" Sauce Powder
- Fat and breadcrumbs

PREPARATION

Cut the prunes into cubes. Drizzle the prunes and raisins with rum and marinate for about 30 minutes. In the meantime, peel the apple, cut out the core and cut the apple halves into cubes. Knead the lemon peel, orange peel, breadcrumbs, flour, fat, brown sugar, lemon zest and juice, eggs, spices and nuts quickly with the dough hook of the hand mixer. Put everything in a greased pudding tin (800 ml) sprinkled with breadcrumbs and press lightly. Close the pudding mold and cook in a hot water bath for 2 hours. Take the pudding out of the water, let it rest for 10 minutes and turn it out of the mold. Let the pudding cool completely for 2 hours. Mix 5 tablespoons of milk and 25 g of sugar with the sauce powder. Bring the rest of the milk to the boil, remove from the stove, stir in the mixed sauce powder and bring to the boil again. Let cool down. Serve the plum pudding with the vanilla sauce

CHOCOLATE CAKE

Servings: 4

INGREDIENTS

- 200 g granulated sugar
- 200 g margarine (or butter)
- 200 g flour (smooth)

- 1 packet of baking powder
- 3 eggs
- 3 tsp cocoa powder
- 3 teaspoons of waterOn the shoppinglist
- Themed worlds
- Baking recipes
- Cakes and pies recipes
- Chocolate recipes
- Cake recipes

PREPARATION

Beat eggs with sugar and butter at room temperature until frothy.

Sieve the baking powder into the flour (this way there are no lumps in the dough). Mix both with the egg mixture.

Mix cocoa with water and fold into the chocolate cake mixture.

Bake the chocolate cake at 160 ° C (hot air) for about 25 minutes.

FILET WELLINGTON

Servings: 4

INGREDIENTS

- 1 package Aunt Fanny Fresh Butter Puff Pastry (270 g)
- 500 g beef lung roast (cut from the center piece)
- 2 tbsp oil

- 250 g mushrooms (finely chopped)
- 3 shallots (sliced)
- 3 leaves of cabbage (blanched)
- 2 tbsp parsley (chopped)
- salt
- Pepper (white)
- 1 egg (for brushing)
- For the sauce:
- 250 ml beef soup
- 1 shallot (finely chopped)
- Butter (cold)
- 20 ml MadeiraOn the shoppinglist
- Themed worlds
- Roast recipes
- Freshly cooked - the best recipes
- Men Cooking Recipes
- roast beef

PREPARATION

For the Wellington fillet, first heat the oil in a pan and sauté the shallots. Add the mushrooms and roast them until there is no more liquid in the pan. Season to taste with chopped parsley, salt and pepper.

Take the butter puff pastry out of the refrigerator approx. 10 minutes before processing and preheat the oven to 210 ° C.

Season the lung roast with salt and pepper and fry vigorously on all sides in hot oil. Lift the meat out of the pan and let cool down completely.

Unroll the butter puff pastry, place the cabbage leaves on the dough, spread the onion / mushroom mixture evenly on the dough, place the lung roast on top and roll up tightly. Seal the ends well, brush with the beaten egg and decorate with leftover dough if necessary.

Bake hot for about 10 minutes, reduce the temperature to 170 ° C and finish baking for about 20-30 minutes. Then cover with aluminum foil and leave to rest for 10 minutes.

For the sauce, sauté the shallot in the roast set from the lung roast. Deglaze with Madeira, add beef soup and reduce. Finally stir in ice-cold butter and do not boil again!

Arrange the fillet Wellington with the sauce and serve.

SHORTBREAD

Servings: 30

INGREDIENTS

- 200 g butter (soft)
- 100 g caster sugar (fine)
- 300 grams of flour

- some saltOn the shoppinglist
- Themed worlds

PREPARATION

For the shortbread, first mix the sugar, flour, salt and butter into a dough. Knead briefly on a floured work surface, then shape into a roll. Wrap in cling film and let rest in the refrigerator for about 60 minutes.

In the meantime, line a baking sheet with parchment paper. Pre-heat the oven to 170 ° C top / bottom heat.

Unwrap the roll and cut about 1 cm wide slices. Alternatively, the dough can be rolled out 1 cm thick and cut into rectangles with a knife.

Place on the baking sheet with sufficient space and prick with a fork. The shortbread push for about 15 minutes in the oven.

FISH AND CHIPS WITH PICADILLY SAUCE

Servings: 4

INGREDIENTS

- 125 g flour
- 150 ml of water
- 1 pinch of salt
- 200 g mayonnaise
- 150 g natural yogurt
- 3 shallots
- 350 g vegetables (pickled in vinegar, e.g.: corn, paprika, cucumber)
- 1 tbsp mustard
- 1/2 tbsp horseradish
- pepper
- 500 g potatoes (waxy)
- Fat (for deep-frying)
- 500 g cod (in pieces)
- Vinegar (for drizzling)

PREPARATION

For the fish and chips, first preheat the oven to 250 ° C. Mix the flour with the water and salt to form a smooth dough and leave to swell for 20 minutes.

In the meantime, mix the mayonnaise and yogurt for the dip. Add the diced shallots and the pickled vegetables, mustard and horseradish and stir in. Season to taste with salt and pepper.

Peel the potatoes, wash them, cut into sticks and dry them well. Heat the fat to 180 ° C and fry the potatoes in portions until they are almost done. Remove, reheat the fat and deep-fry the chips until golden brown. Remove, drain and keep warm in a preheated oven at 225 ° C.

Wash and dry the fish, cut into portions, season with salt and pepper. Pull the fish in portions through the batter, deep-fry until golden brown and drain on paper towels.

Fish and chips are drizzled with dip or vinegar in proper style and served in a newspaper rolled into a bag.

FRUITY BREAD-AND-BUTTER PUDDING WITH CINNAMON CREAM

Servings: 4

INGREDIENTS

For a medium baking dish:

- 200 g brioche (stale, or 4 rolls)
- 250 g apples (instead of apples, plums or apricots)
- 2 tbsp raisins (soaked in brandy or rum)
- 2 tbsp hazelnuts (chopped, or walnuts)
- 200 ml whipped cream
- 200 ml milk (more depending on the dryness of the rolls)
- 2 pc eggs
- Granulated sugar (to taste)
- 1 packet of vanilla sugar
- Lemon peel
- cinnamon
- Butter and sugar (for the mold)
- For the set:
- Whipped cream
- cinnamon

PREPARATION

For the fruity bread-and-butter pudding with cinnamon butter, cut the brioche or bread rolls into slices.

Whisk the whipped cream with milk, eggs, a tablespoon of crystal and vanilla sugar and pour about two thirds of it over it.

Set the rest aside.

Let the mass steep a little.

In the meantime, spread a suitable baking dish - or preferably two small baking dishes - with butter and sprinkle with sugar.

Core the fruit or cut out the core of the apples and cut the fruit into suitable flat pieces, slices or cubes. (Make sure that the pieces do not get too big.)

Mix with the soaked raisins, nuts, cinnamon, a little lemon peel and, if you like, a little sugar.

Preheat the oven to 180 ° C.

Pour half of the breadcrumbs into the mold (s), spread the fruit over it and cover again with the breadcrumbs.

Press everything down well and pour the rest of the icing over it.

Bake in the oven for a good half an hour until golden brown.

AMERICAN APPLE PIE

Servings: 8

INGREDIENTS

- 1250 g apples
- 70 g sugar (brown)
- 1 1/2 teaspoons cinnamon (ground)

- 1/2 lemon For the dough:
- 75 g butter
- 75 g coconut fat
- 300 grams of flour
- 1 teaspoon of sugar
- 1/4 teaspoon salt
- 4 tbsp water (cold)
- 1 yolk
- 1 egg (for brushing)
- some fine granulated sugar (for sprinkling)

PREPARATION

For the American apple pie, first prepare the batter. To do this, knead the butter, coconut fat, flour, sugar and salt until crumbly. Add the water and yolk. Shape the dough into a ball, divide in two and put both in cling film in the refrigerator for about 1 hour.

In the meantime, prepare the filling. To do this, peel the apples and remove the core. Cut into slices that are not too thin. Squeeze the lemon and mix immediately with the apples. Add sugar and cinnamon and mix well.

Preheat the oven to 180 ° C.

Roll out half of the dough thinly and place in a greased pie tin. Spread the filling on top. Brush the edges of the pastry with the beaten egg. Roll out the second half of the dough and place over the filling. Press firmly on the edge. If you still have leftover dough, you can also use it to decorate. Brush the pie with the egg and prick several times with a fork or cut into it with a knife. Sprinkle with the fine granulated sugar.

BASIC CUPCAKES RECIPE

Servings: 12

INGREDIENTS

For the dough:

- 125 g flour
- 1 teaspoon baking powder
- 125 g of sugar
- 125 g butter
- 2 eggs
- 2 tbsp milk
- 1 pinch of salt For the cream (= topping):
- 320 g of icing sugar
- 150 g butter (room temperature)
- 1 packet of vanilla sugar
- 4 tbsp water (hot)

PREPARATION

Prepare the ingredients for the cupcakes, bring the butter to room temperature and let the flour trickle through a sieve so that there are no lumps in the dough.

Preheat the oven to 185 ° C hot air.

Beat the butter and sugar with the mixer until frothy. Beat the eggs and stir well into the dough one at a time. Stir in a pinch of salt. Add the milk and continue to stir everything until frothy. Finally fold in the flour.

Empty the batter into a muffin tray lined with muffin cups. Fill the molds only about 2/3 full.

Bake in the oven for about 12 minutes. Let cool down well, otherwise the cream won't stick.

Then decorate the cupcakes with a cream (= topping) of your choice.

For this "vanilla cream" variant: stir the sugar and butter until foamy and dilute with the water. Apply the cream to the muffins with an injection kit or alternatively with a spoon and decorate with your choice (sugar balls, blossoms, candied fruits, etc.).

RASPBERRY MERINGUE TRIFLE

Servings: 6

INGREDIENTS

- 200 g meringue
- 500 g raspberries (if there are no fresh ones, also with frozen ones)
- 500 ml whipped cream
- Granulated sugar (to taste)
- 4 cl raspberry spirit (or Grand Marnier)

PREPARATION

For the raspberry meringue trifle, beat the whipped cream with sugar almost stiff to taste (the meringues are already sweet, so use sugar sparingly). Roughly crumble half of the meringues in a glass bowl. Spread half of the frozen raspberries on top and drizzle with half of the alcohol. Then distribute half of the whipped cream on top. The remaining half of the ingredients are also layered: meringues, raspberries, alcohol, whipped cream.

Now the whole thing has to go through in the refrigerator for two hours. The raspberries slowly thaw. The raspberry juice and alcohol soak the meringues, while the whipped cream absorbs the cold and freezes slightly.

The whole thing is reminiscent of a sweet, fruity semi-frozen food and is absolutely addictive.

BUTTERMILK SCONES

Servings: 6

INGREDIENTS

- 225 g wheat flour
- 1 pinch of salt
- 1 teaspoon baking powder

- 40 g butter (cold, diced and butter for the pan)
- 100-150 ml buttermilk
- 1 egg (whisked)

PREPARATION

For the buttermilk scones, sieve the flour, salt and baking powder into a bowl. Add the butter and knead the mixture into small crumbs. Add the buttermilk and mix with a palette knife to form a soft, not too sticky dough. Place on a lightly floured work surface, knead again briefly and shape into an approx. 2 cm thick dough base.

Cut out circles with a mold (6 cm diameter) and place them on a baking sheet lightly buttered, making sure there is enough space between them. Brush with the beaten egg.

Bake for about 12–15 minutes until golden brown. Allow to cool on a kitchen rack and serve with jam and the buttermilk scones with plenty of clotted cream (alternatively double cream).

CHILI CON CARNE PIE

Servings: 6

INGREDIENTS

- 1 puff pastry (or 2 large sheets of philo or "puff pastry " dough)
- 1 kg beef (shoulder or neck, cut into small cubes)

- 1/2 teaspoon salt
- Pepper (fresh, black)
- 1 teaspoon oil
- 1 onion (large, finely chopped)
- 1 cinnamon stick
- 5 cloves of garlic (minced)
- 1 tbsp chili powder (hot)
- 1/2 tbsp cumin (grated)
- 2 teaspoons oregano (dried)
- 1 teaspoon coffee powder (up to 2 teaspoons)
- 1 can (s) of tomatoes (small, diced)
- 375 ml chicken soup (approx.)
- 1 can (s) of beans (small, red, washed and drained)
- 1 can (s) corn (small, drained)
- Cheddar (grated)
- some coriander (freshly chopped)

PREPARATION

For the chili con carne pie, heat the oil in a deep frying pan. Add the finely chopped meat and toast until browned. Remove the meat from the pan and set aside.

Put the onions and the cinnamon stick in the pan and let them take on color for about 5 minutes. Add the chilli, oregano, cumin, coffee powder and salt and simmer for 2 minutes. Add the garlic and cook for another two minutes.

Add the diced tomatoes, beans, corn and chicken soup. Simmer gently for 30 minutes, then let the chili con carne cool down.

Press half of the batter into a pie mold and fill it with the chili con carne. Sprinkle with grated cheddar cheese and fresh chopped coriander. Cover with the second half of the dough and press both layers together in a nicely wavy shape.

Prick the center of the pie a few times with a fork to allow hot air to escape while it is baking.

Bake the chili con carne pie in the preheated oven at 180 ° C for 20 minutes.

LEMON MERINGUE PIE

Servings: 6

INGREDIENTS

For the pie dough:

- 400 g of flour

- 6 grams of salt
- 6 grams of sugar
- 225 g butter
- 20 ml ice water (up to 40 ml)
- For the pie filling:
- 6 eggs (large)
- 2 lemon (lemon zest)
- 120 ml lemon juice
- 270 g sugar
- 112 g butter For the meringue topping:
- 8 egg whites (large)
- 170 grams of sugar
- 20 g vanilla sugar
- 150 g Cream of Tatar

PREPARATION

For the pie dough:

Mix the flour, salt and sugar together. Cut the cold butter into small cubes and mix into the flour mixture. Knead quickly and then add the ice water to make a smooth, supple dough. Wrap it in cling film and let it rest in the refrigerator for at least 1 hour.

ATTENTION: Do not stir or knead the dough for too long! The butter flakes should still be preserved. This will make the dough crispier when you bake it.

For the pie filling:

Mix egg yolks, lemon nests, lemon juice and sugar in a saucepan and bring to a simmer. Stir constantly (!!!) so that the mixture does not burn. Cook until the mixture thickens and bubbles form around the edge. Then stir in the butter piece by piece until it has completely melted.

Press the rested dough into a large pie form (approx. 1-1.5 cm thick) and blind-bake in the oven for 20 minutes until it has a light golden color. For blind baking, weigh down the dough with beans or blind baking balls, which are removed again after the baking process.

Pour the cooled lemon mixture into the cooled dough base so that the mold is about half full. Cover with cling film and let cool in the refrigerator for an hour. Make a meringue topping just before serving.

For the meringue topping: Beat

All the ingredients in the mixer with the whisk until stiff.

To finish the lemon meringue pie, take the pie out of the refrigerator, remove the cling film and distribute small cups from the meringue topping on the lemon mixture so that the entire pie is covered.

Finally, flame light brown with a flamer so that the sugar in the topping caramelizes.

Arrange the lemon meringue pie immediately and cut it at the table.

DUMPLINGS WITH MEAT FILLING

Servings: 4

INGREDIENTS

- 500 g of flour
- 150 g butter
- 4 tbsp salt
- 10-12 tbsp water (cold)
- 1 piece of kohlrabi
- 2 pcs. Potatoes
- 1 pc onion
- 450 g beef
- pepper
- salt
- butter
- parsley
- 1 pc egg

PREPARATION

For the dumplings, first prepare the dough. To do this, knead the ingredients into a smooth dough and leave to rest in the refrigerator for at least 1 hour.

In the meantime, cut the kohlrabi, potatoes and meat into cubes.

Roll out the prepared dough and cut out approx. 23 cm circles from it. Divide the ingredients over half of the dough, season and pour a little butter on top. Moisten the corners for a better hold, fold them together and press firmly.

Pierce the surface of the dumplings several times with a fork. Brush the pockets with egg and bake at approx. 200 ° C for approx. 15 minutes. Then reduce the temperature to 180 ° C and bake for another 30-40 minutes.

Take the finished dumplings out of the tube and enjoy them hot.

MINI SCONES WITH STRAWBERRIES

Servings: 10

INGREDIENTS

For the scones:

- 175 g flour
- 1 teaspoon baking powder
- 45 g butter (soft and in small cubes)
- 2 tbsp sugar (fine)
- 1 egg
- 60 ml whipped creamFor the topping:
- 100 ml whipped cream
- 2 tbsp sugar
- 5-10 strawberries
- Icing sugar (for sprinkling)

PREPARATION

Prepare the scones batter for the mini scones with strawberries. To do this, knead the butter with the flour and sugar. Mix the egg with the whipped cream and gradually stir in a little flour until a soft dough forms.

Roll out the dough thinly on a floured work surface and cut out with cookie cutters (e.g. heart shape) and place on a baking sheet with wrapping paper. Bake in a preheated oven at 160 ° C for about 10 minutes.

Beat the whipped cream with the sugar and cut the strawberries in halves or quarters. Spread some of the whipped cream on the cold scones and garnish with strawberries. Sprinkle with icing sugar and arrange the mini scones with strawberries on a platter.

ETON MESS

Servings: 4

INGREDIENTS

- 200 g meringue (wind bakery, bought ready)
- 500 g strawberries
- 250 ml whipped cream

PREPARATION

For Eton-Mess, grind the meringues.

Beat the whipped cream until stiff.

Wash the strawberries, remove the sepals and cut into bite-sized pieces.

Place the meringue pieces in a nice dessert bowl, spread the strawberries on top, add the whipped cream and mix a little.

Decorate the Eton Mess with a mint leaf before serving.

KEDGEREE WITH SMOKED SALMON AND QUAIL EGGS

Servings: 4

INGREDIENTS

- 400-500 g smoked salmon
- 8-12 pieces of quail eggs
- 250 g rice
- 2-3 pcs. Spring onions
- 500 ml water (or clear vegetable soup, possibly half mixed with coconut milk or whipped cream)
- Salt (to taste)
- Pepper (to taste)
- Curry (at will)
- Garam Masala (at will)
- Turmeric (for sprinkling)
- Lemon juice (or lime juice, if you like)
- Butter (or oil for sweating)
- Coriander (freshly chopped, or parsley)

PREPARATION

For the kedgeree with smoked salmon and quail eggs, first finely chop the spring onions and slowly sauté them in a little butter or oil. If you like, add a pinch of curry and garam masala and roast briefly. Then stir in rice, briefly toast and pour some liquid over it. Now cook like risotto, pouring in the liquid several times and stirring often for about 20 minutes.

Shortly before the rice has finished cooking, cook the quail eggs in water for 2-3 minutes until they are waxy (or 3-4 minutes hard). Let cool briefly and carefully peel. Cut the smoked salmon into strips.

Season the cooked rice with salt, pepper and lemon juice and mix in the chopped coriander. Place the smoked salmon strips on top of the rice, covered, briefly warm or pour cold onto the served rice. Halve the lukewarm quail eggs and garnish the kedgeree with them.

Sprinkle the kedgeree with smoked salmon and quail eggs with turmeric or curry.

QUICK BAKED BEANS WITH CRISPY BACON

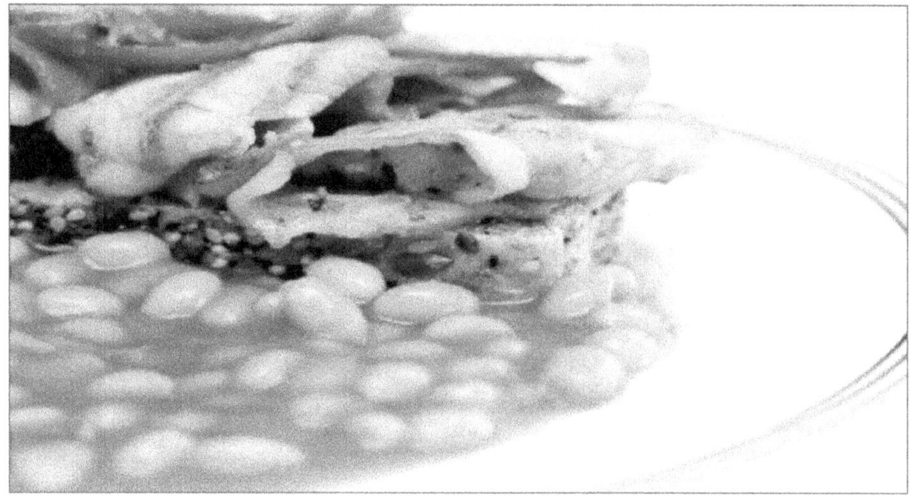

Servings: 4

INGREDIENTS

- 600 g beans (white and canned cooked)
- 8-12 slice (s) of bacon
- 1 pc onion
- approx. 100 ml maple syrup
- 2 tbsp tomato paste
- 1 teaspoon mustard powder (spicy, Colman's mustard powder, alternatively a little more spicy Dijon mustard etc.)
- 150 ml orange or pineapple juice
- 1-2 tbsp brown sugar
- 1 dash of Tabasco sauce (to taste)
- 1 dash of ketchup (to taste)
- pepper
- salt
- 2 tbsp butter
- Oil (for frying)

PREPARATION

For the quick baked beans with crispy bacon, first finely dice the onion and fry it as slowly as possible in hot butter over a mild heat. The onion cubes should be soft at the end, but not too dark. (This makes them taste sweeter.)

In the meantime, stir the mustard powder in a little water or orange juice. Add sugar to the onions and caramelize briefly. Stir in the mixed mustard powder together with the tomato paste and let it boil down briefly. Add the maple syrup and pour a strong dash of orange juice. Salt, pepper and season to taste with ketchup and tabasco sauce. Add the beans and let them simmer for about 20 minutes, until the beans are nice and creamy. (If the baked beans are too dry, add a little water and let the sauce boil down again.)

Meanwhile, regularly cut into the bacon slices at the top edge at finger-wide intervals as desired. Heat some oil in a pan and slowly fry the bacon in it until crispy. Lift out and dab a little with kitchen paper. Serve the quick baked beans with crispy bacon.

BAKED BEANS WITH PORK

Servings: 4

INGREDIENTS

- 300 g white beans (dried)
- 500 g pork (fat, preferably belly meat or streaked bacon)
- approx. 100 ml maple syrup
- 1 teaspoon mustard powder (black, Colman's mustard powder)
- 1-2 tbsp brown sugar
- Ketchup (or tomato paste, to taste)
- pepper
- salt
- Lard (kidney fat)

PREPARATION

For the baked beans with pork, first soak the beans overnight, preferably. Then spread a suitable fireproof pan (with a lid, possibly a Römertopf) with lard and preheat the oven to approx. 170 ° C.

Drain the soaked beans, add some of them to the saucepan, add the meat and group the remaining beans all around. Add enough boiling water to just cover the meat and beans. Cover the pot and cook for 3 ½ – 4 hours until soft, depending on the type of beans (see tip). Meanwhile, stir from time to time and, if necessary, add fresh hot water.

Now stir the mustard powder with a little warm water and mix it with the slightly warmed maple syrup. Season well with salt, pepper and sugar. Stir in ketchup to taste. Lift out the meat, cut into cubes and mix back into the beans. Also stir in the seasoning mixture and cook everything covered again until the beans are almost creamy-soft. Again, if necessary, add more water. Season baked beans with pork and serve with fresh salad and crispy white bread.

FUDGE (ENGLISH CARAMEL CANDY)

Servings: 4

INGREDIENTS

- 250 g couverture (or chocolate)
- 750 g icing sugar
- 225 g butter
- 225 ml whipped cream
- 1-2 tbsp glucose (available from specialist retailers or sugar syrup)
- 2 tbsp corn flakes (crumbled, to taste)

PREPARATION

For the fudge, first line a suitable terrine dish with aluminum foil. Then break the couverture into pieces and place in a saucepan with the sugar, butter and whipped cream. Stir in glucose and slowly bring to the boil over the heat that is not too high. Stir constantly so that the chocolate and sugar can dissolve well.

After the first boil, let it simmer gently for another 5 minutes, stirring repeatedly. Take off the heat again and stir the mixture until it emulsifies nicely, that is, it has become creamy and has cooled down. Stir in the crumbled cornflakes as desired.

Now pour the mixture into the mold and let it cool well in the refrigerator. If possible, cut cold fudge into even pieces or cut out with a spoon.

RHUBARB CRUMBLE

Servings: 4

INGREDIENTS

- 750 g rhubarb
- 2 tbsp pine or pistachio nuts
- 4 tbsp honey

- Sugar as needed
- 1 packet of vanilla sugar
- Rum (to taste)
- 1 tbsp butter (for sweating)
- Butter (for the mold)

For the crumbles:

- 120 g butter
- 120 g granulated sugar
- 150 grams of flour
- 50 g coconut flakes
- 1 pinch of cinnamon

PREPARATION

For the rhubarb crumble, peel the rhubarb sticks (peel off the skin) and cut into pieces. Melt the butter in a saucepan, add the rhubarb and stir briefly. Stir in honey and vanilla sugar and cover and steam the rhubarb until al dente, but not too soft. In between, if necessary, add a little sugar and a little rum to taste. Chop the pine or pistachio nuts, mix in and remove from the heat.

Preheat the oven to 180 ° C. Spread a suitable ovenproof dish with melted butter and pour in the rhubarb. For the crumble, put all the ingredients in a bowl and mix with your hands until crumbly. Spread over the rhubarb and bake the rhubarb crumble in the hot oven for about 25 minutes until golden.

MINCE PIE

Servings: 22

INGREDIENTS

- 1 teaspoon allspice (ground)
- 1 teaspoon salt
- 1 egg yolk (class M)

- 200 g apricots (dried, soft)
- 1 teaspoon of sugar
- 185 g butter (cold)
- 200 ml of water
- 5 tbsp orange liqueur
- Butter (for the molds)
- 2 tbsp water (cold, possibly more)
- 150 g dates (dried)
- 250 g flour
- Flour (for processing)

PREPARATION

First prepare the batter for the mince pie. Chop the butter into small cubes and knead with flour. Add egg yolk, salt, sugar and 2-3 tablespoons of cold tap water and quickly knead together with your hands to form a smooth dough. Shape the dough into a flat brick, wrap it in cling film and let it cool for 1 hour.

To prepare the filling, cut the apricots and dates into 5 mm pieces. Bring 200 ml of tap water to the boil in a saucepan, fold in dried fruits and remove from the kitchen stove. Season the filling with new spices and liqueur and allow to cool.

Roll out 2/3 dough on a floured surface approx. 3 mm thin and pierce approx. 22 circles (7 cm in diameter). Press the dough circles into buttered and floured muffin tins (2 muffin trays with 12 cavities each). Pour 1 tbsp of the filling into each of the wells.

Roll out the remaining dough thinly, cut out 22 circles (each 5 cm ø) one after the other. Poke a small star out of the circles. Put circles on the filling as a lid, press gently until smooth.

Bake in the heated oven on the middle rack from below at 180 ° C (gas 2-3, convection 170 ° C) for 30-35 minutes. Let the pies cool down a little and turn them out of the mold. The mince pie will keep for 1-2 weeks in a tin.